Hike It

An introduction to **camping, hiking, and backpacking** in the U.S.A.

written by
Iron Tazz

illustrated by
Martin Stanev

MAGIC CAT PUBLISHING

Contents

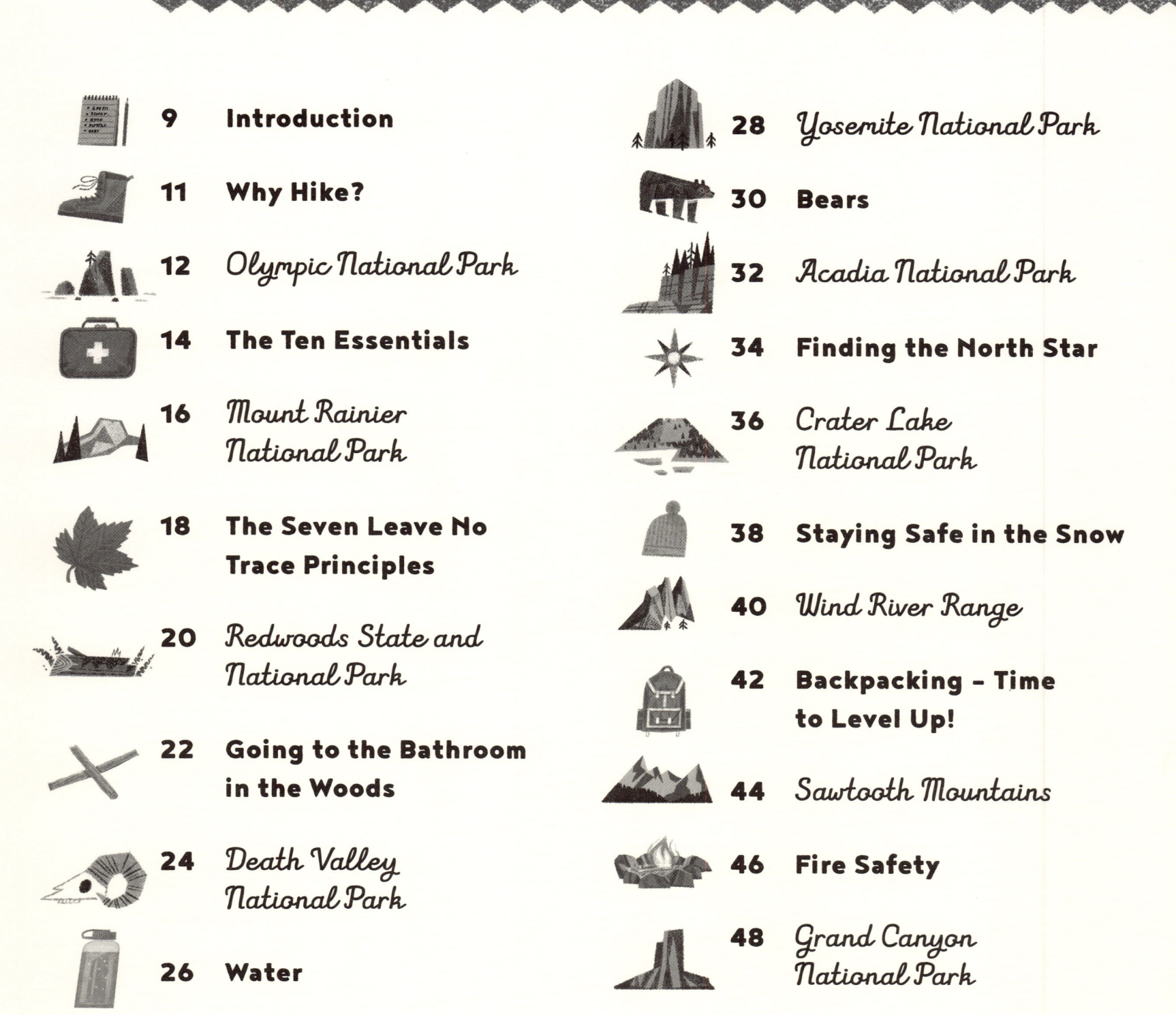

9 **Introduction**

11 **Why Hike?**

12 *Olympic National Park*

14 **The Ten Essentials**

16 *Mount Rainier National Park*

18 **The Seven Leave No Trace Principles**

20 *Redwoods State and National Park*

22 **Going to the Bathroom in the Woods**

24 *Death Valley National Park*

26 **Water**

28 *Yosemite National Park*

30 **Bears**

32 *Acadia National Park*

34 **Finding the North Star**

36 *Crater Lake National Park*

38 **Staying Safe in the Snow**

40 *Wind River Range*

42 **Backpacking – Time to Level Up!**

44 *Sawtooth Mountains*

46 **Fire Safety**

48 *Grand Canyon National Park*

 **50 Navigation Tools and Skills**

 52 *Glacier National Park*

 **54 Wild Berries**

 56 *Arches National Park*

 **58 What To Do If You Get Lost**

 60 *Yellowstone National Park*

 **62 Backpacking Food Guide**

 64 *Great Smoky Mountains National Park*

 **66 Extreme Conditions**

 68 *Petrified Forest National Park*

 **70 Hiking Tips**

 72 *North Cascades National Park*

 **74 Being Mindful in Nature**

 76 *Denali National Park and Preserve*

 **78 Lightweight Backpacking**

 80 *Pacific Crest Trail*

 **82 Thru-Hiking**

 84 *Appalachian Trail*

 **86 Hike Your Own Hike**

 88 *Continental Divide Trail*

 **90 Alright, Little Explorers!**

DISCLAIMER
This book has been made to help you connect with nature.
It is not intended as a survival handbook, so please make
sure you are accompanied by an experienced adult as you
venture into the great outdoors.

Introduction

Simply put, I love hiking and backpacking! I've hiked and backpacked more than 10,000 miles and have spent more than 400 nights in the backcountry . . . These journeys have changed my life for the better in so many ways.

This book aims to open your eyes to the many styles of *hiking* and *backpacking* out there. It will teach you essential skills that will allow you to thrive in the wild, right from your very first day hike . . . Maybe one day you'll even attempt a thru-hike across the entire *United States*! Whatever challenge you take on, I hope this book inspires you to get out in nature and have your own incredible experiences.

The locations in this book are some of the very *best areas* in the USA to hike and go backpacking—they are some of the very best in the world, for that matter!

Besides the long-distance trails, I chose not to recommend specific trails in this book for two reasons. First, this can cause overcrowding (crowded hikes are the worst!) and second, doing a little bit of *research* about an area and picking out the hike that's best for YOU is a fun and essential skill to learn as you progress in your *outdoor adventures*.

So, remember to be prepared, respect the environment, and have fun.

See you on the trail!
Iron

Why Hike?

Something magical begins to happen as you get out on a hike.

My best memories have been made on hiking trips: fishing with friends in wild places, swimming in glacier-fed rivers, catching sunsets on top of mountain peaks, and accomplishing *goals* I never dreamed possible . . . And I've met so many cool, unique trail friends along the way! I am forever grateful to have these *memories* that I can relive again and again.

Your future self will be thankful, too, if you find a *physical activity* that you LOVE! Exercise is key to longevity and a happier, more balanced life. The forests, mountain peaks, and coastlines are my gym.

Most importantly though is the way hiking really draws you into the present. A hike makes you step out of your comfort zone and *disconnect* from everyday life . . . You are gently forced into reconnecting with your inner-self and *nature*, which does *wonders* to support your mental health and creativity. This is where the real magic happens!

Whatever trail I choose, one thing remains consistent: after I finish a hike, I always feel like I level up physically, emotionally, and spiritually.

I never got caught up on the why. I hit the trail and was hooked.

Olympic National Park

If I could only pick one area to hike for the rest of my life, it would be the Olympics.

The amount of land open to backpacking and hiking in Olympic Park is simply amazing, with more than 600 miles of trails and 73 miles of protected coastline along the Pacific Northwest.

As you hike, admire massive sea stacks, driftwood logs the size of buses, ancient trees, bald eagles, sea anemones, and river otters. There are even sacred rock carvings from the Makah Tribe, thought to be up to 500 years old.

With coastal hikes, lush *rainforests*, and *mountain glaciers*, this area has it all.

The Ten Essentials

The Ten Essentials list goes all the way back to the 1930s . . . and it's amazing how relevant this list still is today!

Every hiker should carry the Ten Essentials, no matter how short or easy their hike is. This list might seem excessive for a short day hike, but the goal here is to be prepared for anything. I've seen people get lost on more than one occasion on short hikes, and you never know when you might be able to help someone else on the trail.

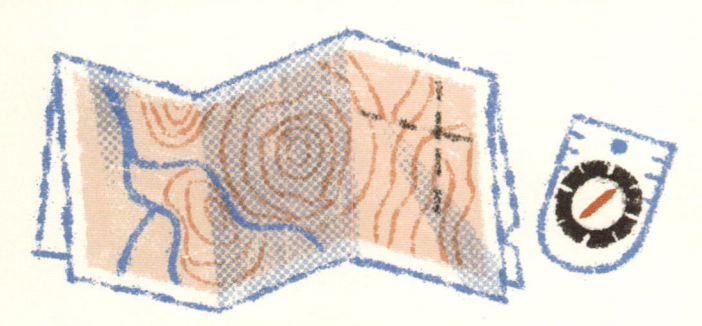

1. Directions
A map, compass, and GPS device can help you stay on track and find your way back to civilization if you get lost.

2. Sun protection
Sunscreen, sunglasses, a hat, and long sleeves will help protect you from the sun's intense rays. I even use an umbrella sometimes when I'm hiking in hot desert areas with no shade.

3. Extra clothing
An extra layer or two such as a fleece or puffy jacket will keep you warm. Bring rain gear if there is a chance of rain.

4. Illumination
A headlamp or flashlight is a must if you're hiking out after sunset. I carry an extra set of batteries, too.

5. First-aid kit
Basic supplies such as bandages, gauze, and pain medication can help you treat minor injuries and ailments.

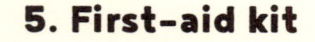

6. Fire starter
A lighter, matches, and a fire starter can help you start a fire for warmth or signal for help in an emergency. I carry two lighters in case one fails or runs out of fuel.

7. Repair kit

A small repair kit with items such as duct tape, super glue, and a knife or multi-tool can help you fix gear that breaks on the trail.

8. Food

Bring more than enough food to keep you energized on your trip. Some people bring an extra day's worth in case they get lost.

9. Water

A water bottle or hydration system will help you stay hydrated on the trail. I also carry a water filter so I can drink wild water without getting sick.

10. Emergency shelter

A small, lightweight tarp or bivouac ("bivy") sack can provide shelter in case of an unexpected overnight stay. Even a couple extra-large garbage bags or an emergency heat blanket can help if you don't have a shelter.

Modern Essentials

There are two other things I consider essential on every hike. Those are...

1. Poop kit

We'll talk more about this later . . . !

2. Cell phone

Having a cell phone can be a lifeline if you get lost (even if you don't have cell service).

I also store maps on my phone and use it as a GPS device. And I love taking pictures on all of my adventures. Remember to put your phone in airplane mode to save battery!

Mount Rainier
National Park

Mount Rainier is the tallest in the Cascade Range and is technically an active volcano!

The last time this mountain erupted was more than 500 years ago; today, you're more likely to find lakes filled with water than lava. In fact, the native Puyallup Tribe's name for Mount Rainier is Tahoma, or Tacoma, which means *"the mother of waters."*

One of the most amazing backpacking trails in the world—the *Wonderland Trail*—circles around this mountain. It's 93 miles long and takes most backpackers one to two weeks to complete.

With more than 275 miles of trails, there are lots of short hike options in the park, too, where you can explore everything from old-growth forests to *wildflower fields*, when hundreds of species burst into life in summer.

The Seven Principles of Leave No Trace

By following these principles we can help protect the natural beauty of our environment, preserving it for future generations. You can be proud to know that you are a responsible steward of the land.

1. Plan ahead and be prepared
Before you go on a nature adventure, make a plan and be ready for anything.

2. Travel and camp on durable surfaces
Help protect the earth by not walking or camping on plants or vegetation. Stick to trails and established campsites when you can.

3. Dispose of waste properly
Pack it in, pack it out. This includes orange and banana peels!

4. Leave what you find
Preserve the park by leaving rocks, plants, and other natural objects as you find them. This includes not building rock stacks.

5. Be careful with fire

Check whether you're allowed to have a fire in that area. If you are, make sure it's in a designated fire pit and keep it small, using little sticks that are already on the ground.

IMPORTANT

Make sure your fire is completely extinguished before leaving camp.

6. Respect wildlife

Enjoy watching animals from afar, but don't feed them or get too close to them.

7. Be considerate of others

When we're outside, there might be other people enjoying nature too. To be respectful, keep voices and noise low to give everyone the chance to enjoy the beauty of nature (loud music can especially crush the vibe!).

Another cool thing to do is pick up any garbage you see on the trail. Picking up a gum or candy bar wrapper is sure to bring good karma your way!

Redwood National and State Parks

Walking among some of the tallest and oldest trees in the world makes the Redwoods one of my favorite places to hike.

It is an amazing feeling to stand next to one of these *giant trees* and look up to the very top, more than 350 feet in the air!

One of the reasons these trees grow so tall is because of all the *fog* that comes off the California coast. This creates some epic hiking conditions: hiking through the mist as rays of light break through the fog is just *magical*.

And with more than 200 miles of trails that weave through diverse environments including prairies, beaches, and stunning spring-time rhododendron blooms, there's something for every season!

21

Going to the Bathroom in the Woods

Many hiking trails and campsites have restrooms. If they do, be sure to use them! If not—and you need to go!—here's my guide.

Poop kit

1. Small sealable bag
To pack out your used toilet paper.

2. Toilet paper
Bring enough for every poop on the trail...

3. Big sealable bag
Store your entire poop kit in here.

4. Hand sanitizer
Use this after every poop stop.

1. Choose your spot
Find a spot at least 200 feet away from any trail, campsite, or water source.

2. Dig a hole
Dig a hole 6 to 8 inches deep. Some hikers bring a small trowel but I just use a trekking pole or a stick.

3. Pop a squat
Pop a squat, and let it rip!

4. Pack it out

Use as little toilet paper as possible and store it in your small sealable bag. You can also use nearby leaves if you're confident they aren't poisonous.

5. Clean your hands

Fill in the hole with dirt to cover it over, then sanitize your hands.

6. Mark the spot

If possible, I put two sticks crossed in an X on top of my filled-in hole. This will signal to the next person not to dig there.

Some sensitive areas require you to pack out human waste. You also have to do this in deep snow where you can't dig down to the dirt. In either scenario, you must pack your poop out in special bags. Fun!

Peeing

Peeing outside is much easier. No hole is needed, just make sure you are at least 200 feet away from any water sources. If you are in a high alpine area, try to pee on rocks instead of vegetation; goats and deer are attracted to the salt in your pee and they will tear up fragile vegetation to get to it.

Death Valley
National Park

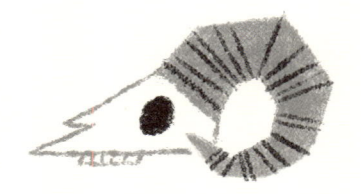

Spanning California and Nevada, this desert is renowned for its dry climate, hot temperatures, and rugged landscapes.

Despite its name, Death Valley is home to a variety of unique plants and animals that have adapted to survive its *harsh environment*. You might see colorful wildflowers blooming in the spring or spot a coyote or a desert tortoise as you explore the park.

Hiking through Badwater Salt Flat takes you 282 feet below sea level, which is the *lowest point* in North America! This massive 200-square-mile salt flat is made up of large polygon salt formations that stretch out as far as the eye can see.

Death Valley also holds the world record for hottest temperature ever recorded: 134 degrees Fahrenheit! Because it gets so *intensely hot* here, the best months to visit are generally from November to April.

The Importance of Water

Dehydration is no joke, especially if you're hiking in hot desert areas like Death Valley or the Grand Canyon.

People die every year from dehydration on the trail. That's the worst-case scenario. Drinking plenty of water is vital for keeping your energy levels up, and learning how to purify wild water is a skill all hikers should have.

How much water should I bring?

As a general rule, bring at least 1 liter of water per person for every hour of hiking. So, bring at least 2 liters of water for a two-hour hike. If you're hiking in really hot or difficult conditions you should double that amount. Better safe than sorry.

Camel–up

Before the hike, chug some water. To make sure you are amply hydrated, check your pee! It should be clearish-yellow and you should be peeing more than six times every 24 hours. Darker pee can be an indication you are dehydrated and need to take on more fluids.

Electrolytes

Think you might get really sweaty!? Salty snacks or electrolyte powders can help replenish electrolytes lost in sweat.

Water filter

Water is surprisingly heavy. Because of this, I always bring my water filter on longer hikes and backpacking trips. It is small and lightweight (easy to carry) and attaches to bottles.

Wild water

You can get really sick from drinking untreated wild water. The good news is that wild water is easy to purify with a water filter. This enables you to safely drink from streams, rivers and lakes.

Yosemite
National Park

Yosemite is a sanctuary for the mind and body.

Waterfalls tumble down the massive granite walls here, which jut straight out of the valley.

Vertical rock formations like El Capitan make the High Sierras of Yosemite one of the most famous places in the world for *rock climbing*—look up and you might even see a climber way high up on a wall out here. There are options from easy to advanced—just remember to apply for a Wilderness Climbing Permit before you arrive.

Another incredible feature of this national park is the *John Muir Trail*. This 211-mile trail passes through Yosemite, Kings Canyon, and Sequoia and most hikers take two to three weeks to complete it. Whatever you choose to do here—hike or climb—one thing is for sure: you'll get an awesome view!

Bears

Imagine this: you're hiking down a trail, come around a corner, and there's a giant bear 10 feet in front of you. Ahh!

I've been in this situation a couple times and let me tell you, it can be kind of scary. For the most part, hiking in North America is safe and animal attacks are very rare, but here are some tips on how to stay safe if you encounter a black bear.

Keep your distance

It's always best to try and keep plenty of distance between you and any wild animals. No matter how tempting it is, never approach them.

Don't run

Did you know bears can run over 30 miles per hour? Never, ever try to run away from a bear!

Stay calm

Try to remain as calm as possible and not make any sudden movements that might startle the bear. Avoid direct eye contact.

Make yourself heard

Raise your hands and talk to the bear in a <u>CALM</u> and assertive voice. Let it know you are a human and not a threat. Detour away slowly, without turning your back. Try to get at least 300 feet away.

Grizzly bears

These same principles can be used for grizzly bear encounters.

That said, if you are hiking in an area with grizzlies, carry <u>BEAR SPRAY</u>.

Grizzlies are generally far more aggressive than black bears.

Before setting out, learn how to properly use your bear spray. Practice removing the safety tab and spraying.

Keep the spray handy while you hike so that you can access it quickly!

The idea is to put a big cloud of spray between you and the grizzly if need be, to deter it from getting too close.

Think ahead

National Park Service recommendations on wild animals vary from park to park, so do your research before you set off.

Acadia National Park

As you hike through the wilderness, the city lights fade away, and the sky comes alive with a brilliant display of twinkling lights.

Cities are one of the main sources of light pollution. The bright lights of buildings and streets overwhelm the darkness of the night sky, making it difficult to see the stars. Most wilderness areas get you away from light pollution, and Acadia, which is on the Maine coast, is one of the best places of all to take in a *starry night sky*.

The vast expanse above you is a reminder of just how small we are in the grand scheme of things, and the stillness of the night brings a sense of *peace* and *tranquillity*. So, pack your bags, hit the trail, and prepare to be awed by the celestial show overhead.

Finding the North Star

Finding the North Star is a simple process that can be done in just a few steps. It can also be an awe-inspiring experience to look up and see one of the most constant stars in the night sky. Here's how to do it in North America:

1. Find the Big Dipper
Locate the constellation Ursa Major, also known as the Big Dipper, which is visible throughout most of North America. Look for a group of seven bright stars that form the shape of a dipper or a ladle.

2. Locate the two pointers
Once you've found the Big Dipper, look for the two stars at the front of the dipper's "bowl" that point towards the North Star. These two stars are called the Pointers, and they point directly to Polaris.

Ursa Major (The Big Dipper)

3. Follow the pointers

Draw an imaginary line through the Pointers and extend it five times the distance between the two stars. The bright star at the end of this line is Polaris, the North Star.

4. Check the position

The North Star forms the end of the handle of the constellation Ursa Minor, the Little Dipper. Its location changes a little bit due to Earth's tilt but it's still relatively close to the celestial north pole.

**Ursa Minor
(The Little Dipper)**

**Polaris
(The North Star)**

People have been navigating by this star for thousands of years. It's the only star that appears to stay in the same spot in the sky and it's visible all night—that's why it's so great to navigate by.

Crater Lake
National Park

I was totally blown away the first time I saw this place and have come back many times since.

Located in the Cascade Mountains of Oregon, Crater Lake is the *deepest lake* in the USA and is known for its crystal-clear blue water.

One of the most exciting things about this lake is that it was formed by a volcano! Long ago, a huge mountain called Mount Mazama erupted and collapsed, leaving behind a massive *crater* that filled with rainwater over time.

While this place is absolutely stunning in the summertime, my favorite time to come here is in early spring when the roads surrounding the lake are still buried in *snow*, making for one of the most beautiful snowshoe routes in the world. Just make sure you come prepared for the cold!

Staying Safe in the Snow

Step into a magical world where everything sparkles . . . Hiking in the snow is like exploring a fairytale land.

Everything just feels so peaceful and quiet when it snows. It's a beauty that's hard to put into words, and I hope you get to experience it first-hand. As well as remembering the Ten Essentials, here are some more tips on staying safe and having the most enjoyable experience in a winter wonderland.

Snowshoes and microspikes
Microspikes slide over the bottom of your boots and give you extra traction on hard-packed snow and ice, while snowshoes are ideal for powder or soft snow.

Sun protection
I got the worst sunburn of my entire life hiking in snowy conditions with no sun to be seen. Snow reflects UV rays so be sure to remember your sunglasses and sunscreen.

Staying warm
It can be much colder hiking in snowy conditions (obviously!), so bring enough warm layers: thermal underwear, fleeces, puffy jackets, a warm hat, and gloves. Make sure you have waterproof boots, too.

Drinking water
If the temperature is below freezing I keep my water bottle inside my backpack wrapped inside some of my extra clothing layers. This will keep it insulated and stop the water from freezing. You can also use an insulated water bottle.

Shed layers

Hiking in the snow can be physically demanding, and it's very easy to break a sweat. Make sure you start taking off layers as soon as you feel a sweat coming on. If you don't, your sweat can get really cold when you stop moving and cause your body temperature to plummet dangerously low.

Wag bag

When you're hiking in fragile alpine environments, you should use a special bag system that you poop in and carry out with you to avoid polluting water sources in the wild.

Avalanche dangers

Make sure to research the area you plan on hiking into online before your trip. If there are any possibilities of avalanches you should make other plans. Avalanches can be deadly, and it's always best to play it safe.

Extending battery life

Batteries can die fast in cold conditions. This is important to keep in mind since you might be navigating with a GPS or taking photos. I keep my phone close to my body for warmth and bring a backup battery to charge my electronics.

Tracks in the Snow

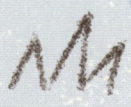

Animal tracks

Keep an eye out for pawprints in the snow. You might spot tracks of rabbits, deer, or even foxes. These tracks tell a story so let your imagination soar. It's like being a snow detective!

Wind River Range

Picture yourself standing amidst tall, snow-capped peaks and vast valleys.

The Winds in western Wyoming boast an impressive network of hiking trails which wind through a world of beautiful lakes and sparkling rivers. *Wildlife* is everywhere: look out for majestic elk, playful marmots, and soaring eagles.

As you pass through forests of tall *pine trees*, listen to the gentle rustling of leaves and melodic *birds* chirping overhead. You'll likely come across one of the many rivers here, perfect for splashing your feet and cooling off.

Hiking here is not only exciting, but it also teaches us important lessons about nature and the *environment*. As we walk on the trails, we understand how the mountains provide fresh air, clean water, and a sanctuary for wildlife.

Backpacking—Time to Level Up!

Carrying everything you need to survive in the wilderness on your back is the ultimate adventure and is one that will stay with you long after you leave the trail.

Once you are self-sufficient, you can get to places that can't be reached on a day hike. The right equipment is essential for staying safe and having a great time on these longer hikes. So, let's talk gear! Here is the stuff you need in addition to the Ten Essentials.

Backpack
Choose one that fits well and has space for all your gear, food, and water. Bring a garbage bag to line the inside of your pack and a pack cover to protect the contents from rain.

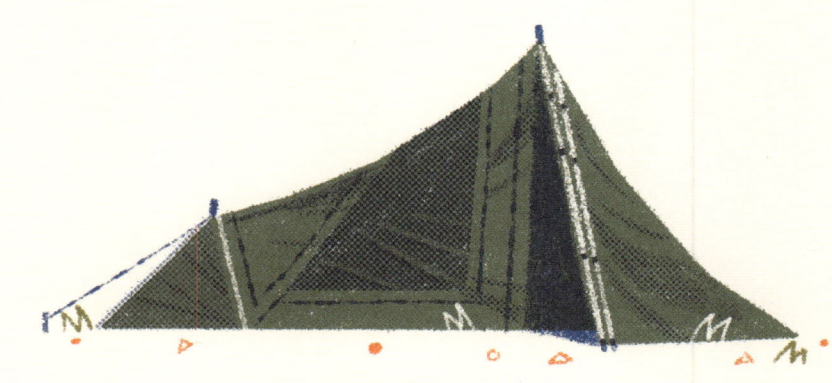

Shelter
This could be a tent, a tarp, or a bivy sack. Make sure your shelter can handle any weather conditions you might encounter and has more than enough space for you and your gear.

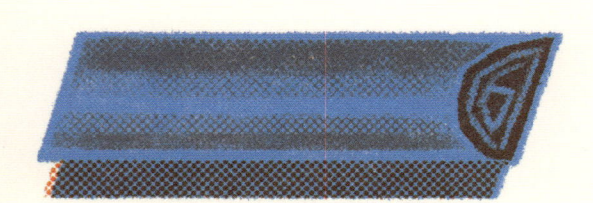

Sleeping pad
I use a compact air mattress. It's comfy and insulates me from the cold ground. You can also use a foam pad.

Sleeping bag or quilt
Choose something warm enough! A bag rated for 20 degrees is a good all-around rating for most hikes.

Stove and cooking supplies

Take a stove, fuel, pot, and spoon at the bare minimum. You can get much more creative here if you want!

Proper footwear

Trail running shoes or boots that fit well are really important. Hiking socks also offer extra padding for added comfort and protection.

Luxury items

Most hikers bring a few non-essentials, such as a camp chair, trekking poles, photography gear, a book, journal, fishing pole, or hammock. The sky's the limit here . . . Just remember you have to carry it all!

Proper clothing

Choose the clothes you hike in carefully. Make sure to have insulating layers and rain gear.

Water filter

Make sure you have a way to treat wild water.

Sharing is caring

Hiking with friends or family? Sharing a tent, cooking supplies, or a water filter will help keep your pack lighter.

Sawtooth Mountains

Pristine lakes and massive boulders dot the Idaho landscape here, where the peaks of the Sawtooth Mountains jut out of the ground like skyscrapers in a city.

This place reminds me to be thankful we have so many *protected natural areas* in the U.S. to explore. We hear a lot about the national parks but there are so many amazing hiking opportunities in the national forests, national monuments, Bureau of Land Management (BLM) land, and state parks, too.

Even though some of these areas are right next to each other, they can have completely different *rules* on things like backpacking permits, bringing your dog on the trail, or car camping, so make sure to check before heading out.

Fire Safety

Telling stories around a campfire with friends, cooking food over an open flame, drying out wet gear, and warming your hands . . . A fire can feel like pure magic on a hike.

I'm pretty sure I won my fiancé over by cooking her teriyaki chicken over a fire on our first backpacking date! But while it's magical to enjoy campfires like our ancestors, we have to stay mindful that fires can be wildly destructive. As Smokey Bear says, "Only you can prevent wildfires." So, here are some tips to keep you safe.

Before your trip
Fires are a no-go in many fragile ecosystems and high-elevation areas. Check the regulations to see if campfires are allowed where you plan on camping and make sure there are no burn bans.

Leave no trace
Use existing fire pits where they are available. Keep fires small and only use dead wood that's already fallen on the ground.

Care for live trees

Never cut down live trees or branches. This can this be devastating to an ecosystem.

Wet conditions

Starting a fire in wet conditions can be challenging, so pack a few extra fire starters and a knife or hatchet to cut the wood into smaller pieces.

Fire starting tips

Take the time to collect more than enough tinder and smaller pieces of wood before trying to start a fire.

Completely put out a fire

Never leave a fire until it's completely put out. Embers and sparks are enough to cause a fire to restart, with potentially devastating consequences.

Grand Canyon National Park

There's no better way to appreciate this massive landscape than on a hike!

The Grand Canyon is 278 miles long and more than 18 miles across at its widest point. It is considered one of the *Seven Natural Wonders of the World*.

There are so many awesome trails here: you can hike way down to the *Colorado River* or enjoy a stroll along the top. The Rim-to-Rim Hike is a round trip that is almost 50 miles in length and no easy feat. Still, you can take a much shorter hike on the South Rim, which has many amenities for visitors, or escape the crowds at the North Rim, which gets far fewer visitors and is more than 1,000 feet taller than the South Rim.

Be sure to come *prepared* whichever you choose: more than 250 people get rescued from the Grand Canyon every year!

Navigation Tools and Skills

Be a smart hiker! It's easier than you think to get lost.

I carry a map, compass, and GPS device on all of my hikes. Take the time to learn how to use these tools BEFORE your first hike. Not only is navigating an essential skill, it's also really fun and will have you feeling like a true explorer in no time. It can be tempting to use your phone or GPS device solely, but they can break or malfunction, or run out of battery, so you need a back-up. Don't rely on technology: here are the essentials you need to navigate.

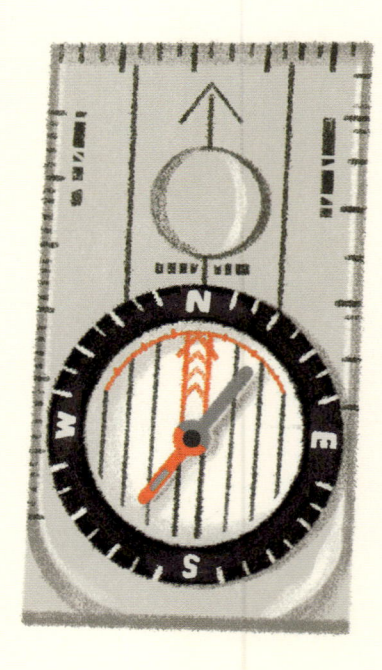

A map
Get a paper map to the area you will be hiking and store it in a sealable bag to keep it dry.

A GPS device
I use a GPS app on my phone. I always make sure to download the maps I need before my hike. Some hikers prefer a dedicated GPS device.

A compass
Choose a compass that allows you to adjust its declination (see box on opposite page).

How to use a map and compass

1. Pick a waypoint

Make sure you have a detailed map of the area you're in. Lay it flat. Note where you are on the map (location A) and a waypoint in the direction of where you want to go (location B).

2. Align the compass

Draw a line connecting A to B. Position the long edge of your compass alongside the line, with your direction of travel facing forwards (towards location B).

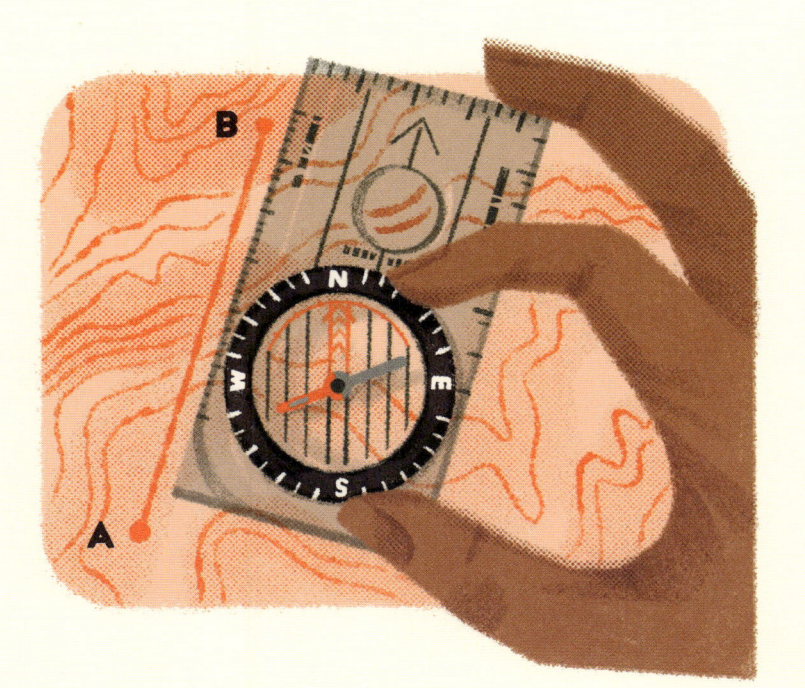

Declination

Declination needs to be adjusted on a compass because it accounts for the difference between true north (the Earth's geographic North Pole) and magnetic north (the direction a compass needle points). By changing the declination, you ensure accurate navigation by aligning your compass readings with true north as indicated on a map. It's a tricky skill to learn but is key to accurate navigation!

3. Align to grid north

Hold your compass in place and twist the dial until 'N' aligns with north on the map.

4. Adjust the declination

'Magnetic north' should be listed on your map. The number will be positive (east) or negative (west). Adjust your declination acordingly. If east, increase; if west, decrease. Verify alignment with true north after adjustment.

5. Turn your body

Pack away your map. Hold your compass flat in front of you. Turn around until your red needle is in the red outline arrow. We call this 'red in the shed'.

6. Set off in the direction of the arrow

The big arrow is now pointing towards your direction of travel. Set off towards your waypoint (location B) and take breaks to check your compass and map.

Practice

Practice using a map and compass in familiar places first and consider learning from experienced navigators or taking a navigation course to improve your skills.

Glacier National Park

Welcome to the northern reaches of Montana, where everything is epic!

Known for its rugged mountains, pristine lakes, and, of course, *glaciers*, this park boasts more than 700 miles of hiking trails and offers amazing options for hikers of all skill levels.

The northern terminus (end) of the 3,100 mile-long *Continental Divide Trail* (CDT) can also be found here, providing an epic backdrop to the final stages of an amazing feat of endurance.

Glacier National Park shares a border with Canada's Waterton Lakes National Park, and together, they form the world's first *International Peace Park*, symbolizing the friendship between the two nations.

53

Wild Berries

The best hikes end with colorful stained hands! Wild berries are nature's candy, and the best part is they're free and packed with nutrients.

Sweet, juicy, plump, and tart, berries have been used as food and medicine for thousands of years. They're a delicious trailside treat and are quite possibly a life-saving food if you get lost. That said, there are many poisonous berries out there, so <u>never, ever eat berries or any wild foods unless you are one hundred percent sure what they are</u>.

Pick up a field guide to learn more, or ask someone who's an expert to help you identify them. Here are some of the more common berries:

Blueberries

Raspberries

Small, intensely flavored berries that thrive in natural, acidic soils and are cherished for their sweet and tangy taste.

Delicious, ruby-red berries found in a variety of habitats, celebrated for their sweet, juicy, and slightly tart flavor.

Huckleberries

Small blue, red or purple berries found in the western United States and Canada, known for their tangy, slightly sweet taste.

Salmonberries

Vibrant, yellow-to-red berries native to North America's Pacific Northwest that are prized for their unique, tart-sweet flavor.

Trailing Blackberries

Also known as dewberries. Low-growing, thorny plants that produce small, black, and sweet berries often found trailing along the ground in sunny, open areas.

Thimbleberries

Known for their delicate, raspberry-like appearance and their sweet-tart flavor. They resemble a thimble that you can put on the end of your finger!

Himalayan Blackberries

Vigorous, thorny shrubs known for their large, juicy, and sweet-tasting blackberries, but they're also considered invasive wherever they are found in the US due to their rapid spread.

Arches
National Park

This park is home to more than two thousand natural sandstone arches, meaning it has the highest concentration of natural arches in the world.

Now you're in eastern Utah, where the rock formations take on wild shapes and sizes: windows, fins, spires, and weathered rock spires. I'm always amazed by the balanced rocks, where massive boulders seem to *defy gravity* by precariously balancing atop smaller pedestals!

Hiking around these other-worldly rock creations might have you thinking you're on Mars or another planet! But these stunning rock formations were created through natural processes here on Earth; *wind, water*, and *ice* have eroded the red Entrada and Navajo Sandstone over millions of years to produce these unique *geological formations*.

What To Do If You Get Lost

Ahh! Getting lost can be downright terrifying. And it happens to thousands of hikers in the USA every year.

One time, I was hiking off-trail with my dad on a cold, rainy October day. Long story short: we got separated, and he got lost. It was one of the scariest nights of my life. My dad didn't have his phone or the Ten Essentials with him. Luckily, I was able to call search and rescue, and they found him safe in the early hours of the morning.

Three lessons I learned from this experience:

1. We shouldn't have *become separated*.

2. We both should have been carrying the *Ten Essentials*.

3. We should both have had our *phones*.

Share your plans

Always let someone know your exact hiking plans before your trip. That includes the route and when you plan on being back. They can alert search and rescue if you aren't back in time.

It's a given to check your map and GPS when lost. Next, remember the *STOP* acronym. This will help you remember how to respond if you think you are lost.

STOP · **T**HINK
OBSERVE · **P**LAN

Stop

The second you realize you're lost, STOP moving. This prevents you from getting further off-course and makes it easier for search and rescue to find you. Take deep breaths and try to relax.

Think

Think about your situation. Consider where you last knew your location, how you got to your current point, and any landmarks or trail markers you remember passing.

Observe

Closely observe your surroundings. Look for landmarks, natural features, or any markers that might help you determine your location.

Plan

Make a plan of action. Decide whether to retrace your steps to the last known point or stay put and signal for help.

If you try to retrace your steps for more than 30 minutes but feel even MORE lost at this point, it's wise to stop and prioritize water, shelter, and how you can signal for help. Most people can survive about 30 days without food and 3 days without water.

Yellowstone National Park

In 1872, Yellowstone was the first national park in the world to be created.

Yellowstone served as a model for the establishment of *national parks* and protected areas worldwide.

Linking Montana, Idaho, and Wyoming, this place is home to more than half of the world's *geysers* (over 10,000!) as well as other geothermal features such as hot springs, fumaroles, and mudpots.

Yellowstone is also home to hundreds of species and is considered by many to be one of the best places in North America to view *wildlife*, with bears, big cats, herds of bison and elk, as well as wolf packs prowling its grasslands.

As the founders of this park imagined more than 150 years ago, this place is truly WILD!

Backpacking Food Guide

I love getting my food ready before I hit the trail! The right foods can make or break a trip but figuring that out is only half of the equation . . .

Unless you want mice chewing through your tent or surprise visits from bears in the middle of the night, it's important you learn how to store your food properly. I'm proud to say that after over a decade of hiking and backpacking, I have never had any animal get to my food.

If your food can hit these marks you are going to be loving life on the trail. . .

Lightweight
Leave the canned goods at home. Try to limit carrying any foods that contain water. Dehydrated and freeze-dried meals are your best friends. This is especially important on longer multi-day trips.

Calorie-dense
Choosing foods with a high calorie density is the easiest way to get your food's weight down. Nuts, nut butters, seeds, trail mix, olive oil, and energy bars are great examples of calorie-dense foods.

Space efficient
Repackaging food such as macaroni into plastic baggies can really help. I save and reuse my baggies for the next trip.

Quick and easy to cook
After a full day's hiking, easy meals that just require water and maybe some olive oil to boost calories are the best. Throughout the day, I just snack. This keeps things simple and means I don't need as much cooking fuel.

Food storage

If an animal can't smell your food, you're winning the game. I always store my food in ODOR-PROOF plastic sealable bags. These don't cost much, come in various sizes, and are worth their weight in gold. First line of defense!

Food dehydrator

I've cooked and dehydrated hundreds of meals and snacks with my food dehydrator over the years. This is a great option that will save you money in the long run and give you more control over what you eat.

Backpacking in an area with bears?

If so, you have a few options for storage at camp: you can store your food in a bear-proof canister, bear-proof kevlar bag, or hang it 12 feet high from a tree. Store any other scented items with your food (such as chapstick, sunscreen, and so on). Check the park regulations before your trip: many areas require the use of a bear can.

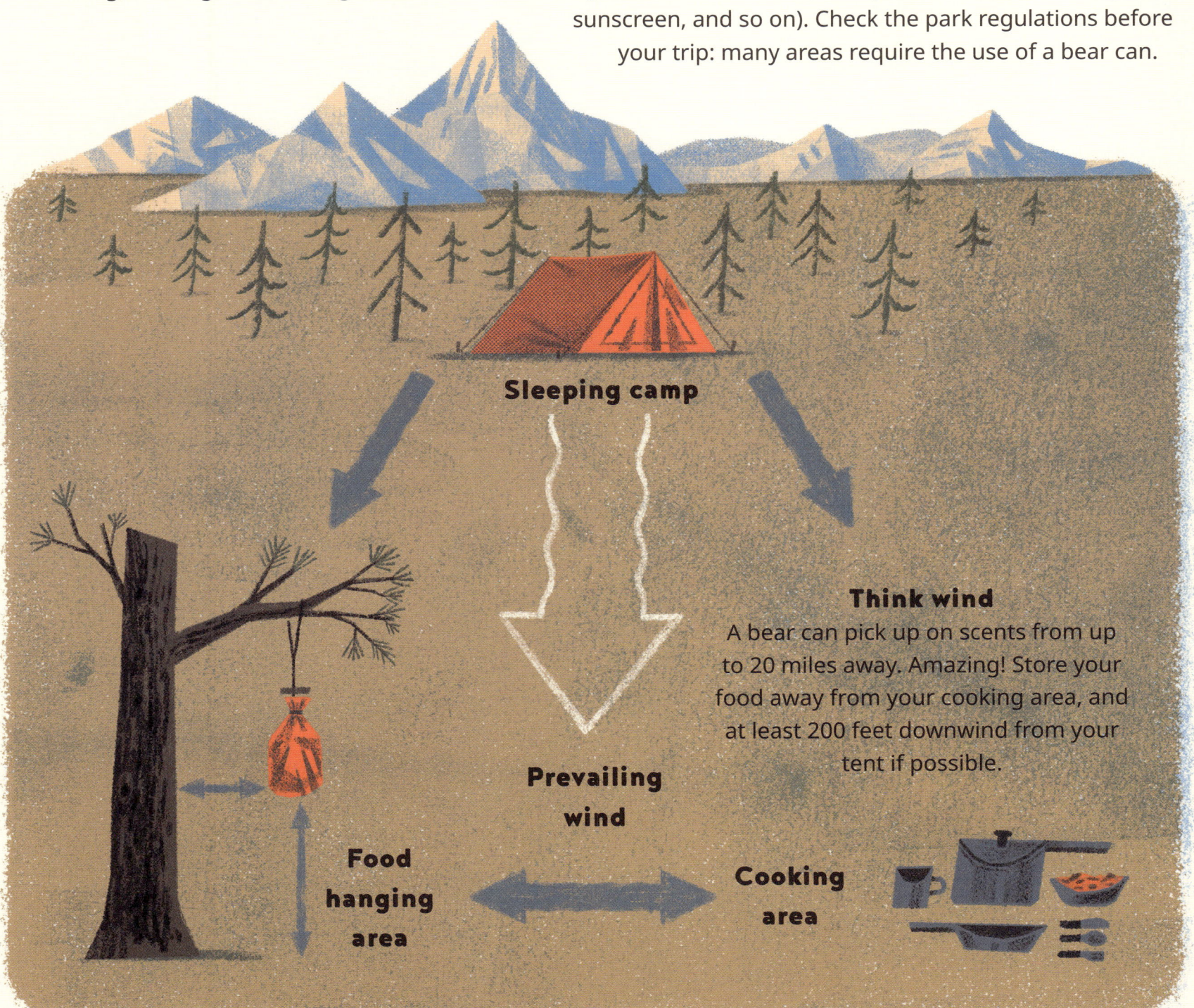

Sleeping camp

Think wind

A bear can pick up on scents from up to 20 miles away. Amazing! Store your food away from your cooking area, and at least 200 feet downwind from your tent if possible.

Prevailing wind

Food hanging area

Cooking area

Great Smoky Mountains National Park

This area between North Carolina and Tennessee gets its name from the mist-like clouds or "smoke" that often shroud the region.

In other words, this park has epic hiking conditions . . . but don't forget your *rain gear*!

The *Appalachian Trail* cuts right through this region. And that's a small part of the 850 miles of trails in this park.

Come here in the fall and be astounded by the tree canopy's of rainbow colors, or in early summer, when a rare species of *firefly* (*Photinus carolinus*) puts on a captivating light show. Thousands of fireflies synchronize their flashing patterns together . . . Prepare to be stunned!

Extreme Conditions

I've hiked in 100-degree heat, battled torrential downpours, been caught in lightning storms and been swarmed by mosquitoes.

There's nothing like being ready for anything and overcoming a challenge! Let's talk about some of the wild conditions hikers encounter and how to be best prepared for them.

Positive attitude

Cultivating a positive attitude when times are tough is essential. Try to remain calm and optimistic no matter how challenging the circumstances are.

Heat

Stay hydrated. Take electrolytes. Wear protective clothing and sunscreen. Take breaks during the hottest part of the day. Choose camps close to water sources.

Heavy rain

Hiking in the rain for days at a time is tough. Use a pack cover and line the inside of your pack with a garbage bag to keep your gear dry. Bring an extra set of warm base layers and save them for sleeping in.

Mosquitoes

A mosquito head net is a must. I cover my body with as much protective clothing as possible. Bug sprays can be really toxic, so I try to avoid them if possible.

What to do in a lightning storm

If you hear thunder, take cover immediately. If you can't find shelter, remain calm but act immediately to avoid being struck by lightning. Here are some steps you can take to stay safe:

Get off of high ground
Lightning is attracted to high points, so it is important to descend from any peaks or ridges.

Seek shelter
Try to find shelter in a stand of small trees or a dry ditch. Avoid tall, isolated trees which could be struck.

Avoid water
Lightning can travel through water, so avoid standing near bodies of water or in puddles.

Stay away from metal objects
Metal objects such as poles and fences conduct electricity; stay at least 100 feet away from them.

Stay low to the ground
Squat, place your hands over your ears, and keep your feet together to make yourself a smaller target.

Stay alert and keep an eye on the storm
Keep an eye on the storm and be ready to move to a safer location if necessary.

Petrified Forest National Park

Welcome to a living museum where you can see towering logs of ancient trees that have been transformed into stone over millions of years.

This area is home to one of the world's largest concentrations of colorful *petrified wood*. Entire petrified trees lay on the ground here and the region's geology, biology, and history are all on display for visitors to explore.

It might be tempting to put a piece of petrified wood in your pocket . . . In the 1930s, visitors began to report that they were *cursed* with bad luck after taking petrified wood from the park! Some say this curse continues today and it is now a part of the park's history. Whether or not taking rocks spells bad fortune for you, it's certainly damaging to the park. So it's especially important you remember one of the *Leave No Trace* principles: leave what you find!

Hiking Tips

Sometimes the little things can make or break your trip.

Imagine trying to enjoy a hike when every steps hurts because massive blisters are forming on your feet. Or instead, sitting by camp after an epic day of hiking, surrounded by wildflowers at peak bloom as you prepare your delicious dehydrated dinner. The second experience is what I like to aim for. Here are my top tips that aren't covered anywhere else in this book!

Start small

Start with short, easy day hikes and progress from there. Same thing for backpacking. I've seen too many people have bad experiences attempting too difficult of a trip at first. Remember, you will have a lifetime to work your way up!

Foot care

Blisters can quickly ruin a trip! Carry a blister kit. Trim your toenails before you hike. Take off your shoes and socks during breaks to let things air out, and keep a pair of dry socks just for sleeping to help your feet dry out and recover overnight.

Try trail running shoes

Outside of winter hiking, I choose trail runners over boots. These shoes are far more comfortable, breathable, and less likely to give you blisters.

Test new gear at home

Gear failures during a trip can be devastating. Soak your tent with a hose at home. Test your rain gear. Break in your new hiking shoes before you leave.

Create a gear checklist

I once went backpacking with a friend and he forgot his tent! Stuff like this happens to the best of us. I run through a checklist before all of my trips.

Choose destinations wisely

Ask yourself: What's the weather going to be like? When are the mosquitoes going to be present? When are the wildflowers going to be at peak bloom? It's fall, so where could I see some awesome fall colors?

Type II fun

Hiking can be hard—physically and mentally. When you're having a tough time, remember that it will pass and often these tough times make the best memories and turn into great stories. We call this Type II fun. Not fun during—but fun looking back!

Keep learning

Remember, the most valuable thing in your tool kit is inside your head. No amount of gear can change that. This book is a great starting point, and I hope it inspires you to read more widely and learn in-depth skills about navigation, fire, foraging . . .

North Cascades National Park

The North Cascades are absolutely jaw-dropping. This area was my gateway into hiking and where I fell in love with being on the trail.

When I imagine this park in Washington State, I think of *waterfalls* forming in magical pools, endless mountain peaks, bears meandering across meadows sprinkled with wildflowers in summer, and larch trees turning from green to brilliant gold in fall.

This area is one of the most *biodiverse* regions in the U.S., hosting an abundance of plants and animals. It also boasts the highest concentration of glaciers in the lower 48.

I love hiking to the historic fire lookouts here; you can even stay in *overnight* in a few of them!

Being Mindful in Nature

Building mindfulness while hiking helps us connect with ourselves and appreciate the beauty around us.

It brings calmness, gratitude, and happiness. It lets us enjoy the present moment and find peace in nature. It's like taking a relaxing break for our minds. Practicing the following things from time to time on your hikes comes with huge rewards, and the peace and insights you experience will last long after your hike!

Step with awareness

Pay attention to each step you take. Feel the ground beneath your feet. Be present in the moment.

Nature's symphony

Listen to the beautiful sounds of nature while you hike. Close your eyes and focus on the songs of birds, rustling leaves, or the wind whispering through the trees.

Observe your surroundings

Look around and notice the wonders of nature. Spot the vibrant flowers, watch squirrels playing, or observe the shapes of clouds in the sky. Every detail is unique and special.

Breathe deeply

Take deep breaths of fresh air as you walk. Feel the air fill your lungs and notice how it feels when you exhale. Breathing deeply helps you relax and stay connected to your surroundings.

Silent walking

Try walking silently for a few moments. Pay attention to the sounds your footsteps make and how your body moves. Connect more deeply with yourself.

Mindful snack time

Eat mindfully. Observe the colors, smells, and textures of your food. Chew slowly and savor every bite. It helps you appreciate the nourishment nature provides.

Tree hugging

Find a friendly tree and give it a gentle hug. Feel the roughness of the bark against your skin. Share your energy with the tree, just as it shares oxygen with you. It's a lovely way to feel connected to nature.

Cloud watching

Lie down on a soft spot and watch the clouds drift by. Notice their different shapes and let your imagination run wild: what could they be? Animals? Castles? Enjoy the peaceful moment.

Gratitude practice

Think about things you're grateful for: beautiful scenery, good health, or the company of loved ones. Let your heart fill with joy. This is my favorite practice of all!

Reflect

At the end of your hike, find a quiet spot to sit and reflect on the sights, sounds, and feelings you've experienced. Appreciate your journey and the mindfulness you cultivated along the way.

Denali
National Park and Preserve

Denali means the "great one" or "tall one" in Athabaskan languages, reflecting the mountain's significance to native Alaskan cultures.

Now we are WAY up north in *Alaska*. Here—as with all the National Parks—we're stepping on traditional Indigenous lands, which contain thousands of years' of Native American history.

In fact, this park alone is at the intersection of five *Indigenous groups*: the Ahtna, Dena'ina, Koyukon, Upper Kuskokwim, and Tanana peoples. Many stories passed down from one generation to the next feature the wildlife here including bear, caribou, and salmon, as well as the ever-present Denali Mountain itself. Rising to 20,310 feet, this is North America's tallest mountain.

Northern Lights, wide open tundras, grizzly bears . . . This area isn't for the faint of heart! And yet, it is a *paradise* for adventurers and the many Alaskan Natives who continue to uphold their cultural traditions here.

Lightweight Backpacking

**Struggling on the trail with way too much gear . . .
A scenario I see often.**

When I hiked the Pacific Crest Trail, my backpacking gear only weighed about 10 pounds. And I had everything I needed to trek for many months in any weather conditions. Lightweight backpacking isn't just for thru-hikers doing these long-distance trails. So many backpackers struggle because they are carrying too much weight. These principles can be used on any backpacking trip.

A light base weight enables you to:
- Hike more miles and experience back-to-back days of JOY
- Carry more food on longer trips
- Bring more luxury items
- Hike more safely across log crossings, creek fords, or uneven ground

Don't go too light!
It might be tempting to leave your first aid kit behind because you rarely use it, but ALWAYS make sure you have the Ten Essentials at the very least.

The Big Three

Your backpack, tent, and sleeping system are usually the heaviest items in your kit. Choosing lightweight gear here will help you tremendously. My two-person tent, tent stakes, sleeping quilt and air mattress only total up to about 6.5 pounds.

Multipurpose gear

My cooking setup is a good example of being multipurpose: I bring just a pot and long-handled spoon. I can eat meals and drink warm drinks from my pot and my spoon works great for everything: no need for an additional cup, bowl or fork. I also use an app on my phone instead of bringing a physical book. And my tent utilizes my trekking poles instead of dedicated tent poles.

Minimize

Take the essentials and nothing else. Take note of things you never use on your trips and next time, leave them behind.

Pacific Crest Trail

The Pacific Crest Trail might be the most beautiful long-distance trail in the world.

Stretching 2,650 miles from Mexico to Canada, through California, Oregon, and Washington, it takes most hikers about five to six months to complete the entire trail. This adventure requires physical fitness, mental toughness, and a strong sense of purpose as you pass through *26 national forests* and seven national parks.

I had never even completed an overnight backpacking trip when I decided I was going to hike the *PCT* (as hikers know it). I gave myself one year to get ready, plan, and learn how to backpack. It was the most inspiring and life-changing thing I've ever done.

You can get a taste of the PCT by taking on a short section of it. This trail even passes through some of the locations mentioned in this book.

Thru-Hiking

Hiking an end-to-end long distance trail like the PCT is called thru-hiking.

Thru-hikers experience some pretty unique things on their long journeys. Backpacking goes from being a fun activity to a way of life. You're on the trail for weeks, so being prepared is essential!

Planning

Leaving your family and all of the comforts of home can be challenging. You also need to get all of the gear and save up enough money for months' worth of food, multiple pairs of shoes, and anything else needed on the trail.

Resupply points

These would be any places you could ship packages to close to the trail or (if you're lucky) a real grocery store. And if there is a diner there, I'm ordering everything on the menu! Thru-hiker hunger is no joke.

Food drops

On the PCT, I would ship boxes full of food to post offices that accepted packages close to the trail. I would typically carry about 5-7 days' worth of food at a time. A lot of my planning was figuring all of the logistics here before the hike.

Shoes

I wore through five different pairs of shoes when I hiked the PCT. This is typical for most thru-hikers.

Trail angels

These beautiful souls are volunteers who help out thru-hikers. They might be posted up at a trailhead barbecuing food for hikers, giving rides into town so hikers can pick up their resupplies, or even letting hikers shower at their houses.

Trail names

Most thru-hikers adopt trail names like Sunshine, Karma, Swammi, or Red Beard – often something connected with a hiking experience. My real name (Iron) sounds like a trail name, so everyone just assumed it was one... And I went with it!

Trail family

The thru-hiking community is wonderful. Sometimes, you hike for days and days together, forming friendships that can last a lifetime.

Appalachian Trail

The Appalachian Trail is one of the most popular long-distance hiking trails in the world and is considered a rite of passage for many hikers.

The *AT* (as it's known) passes through fourteen states on the East Coast of the United States, from Springer Mountain in Georgia to Mount Katahdin in Maine. It typically takes five to seven months to complete the entire trail, depending on the hiker's pace and the time of year.

It's world-famous thanks to its beautiful, varied scenery of *forests*, mountains, and streams.

Hiking the Appalachian Trail is a challenging and rewarding experience that requires physical endurance, mental toughness, and a love of the outdoors. The key to completing this trail— and every other—is to hike your own hike.

Hike Your Own Hike

"Hike Your Own Hike" is a popular saying and mindset among hikers.

The saying encourages you to embrace your own unique hiking style without feeling pressured to conform to societal norms or other hikers' expectations. "HYOH" recognizes that every hiker is different, and there's no one "right" way to hike!

Hike Your Own Hike promotes several key principles:

Individuality

Each hiker has different goals, abilities, and reasons for being on the trail. Maybe you're seeking solitude and a meditative experience; others might want to connect with fellow hikers or prioritize challenging themselves physically. Stay true to your own motivations on the trail!

Pace

Some hikers might prefer to cover long distances each day, while others take a more leisurely approach, stopping frequently to enjoy the scenery or rest. That's perfectly okay. Hiking your own hike means moving at a pace that suits you best without feeling pressured to keep up with others.

Gear and style

Some hikers may choose to carry minimal equipment, while others prefer more comfort items. Select the gear and approach that aligns with your needs and comfort levels and don't feel compelled to follow others.

Flexibility

Stay open to adjusting your plans as circumstances change. Whether it's due to weather, health, or unexpected opportunities, being adaptable allows you to make the best of your experience without rigidly sticking to a plan.

Respect for others

While HYOH celebrates individuality, it also emphasizes respecting the choices and preferences of fellow hikers. Just as you have the right to hike in your unique way, others have the same privilege. Encourage and support others in their hiking journey.

Enjoyment and fulfillment

Ultimately, HYOH encourages hikers to find joy, fulfillment, and a sense of accomplishment in their hiking adventures! By focusing on what brings meaning to your hiking experience, you're more likely to forge unforgettable memories and create a positive impact on your well-being.

HYOH is not just limited to hiking. It can apply to many aspects of life. Embracing the philosophy allows individuals to be true to themselves, confident in their choices, and celebrate their unique journey, both on and off the trail. So, whether you're exploring the wilderness or navigating the twists and turns of life, remember to Hike Your Own Hike!

Continental Divide Trail

Raw, wild, and remote!

The Continental Divide Trial (CDT) traverses 3,100 miles from Mexico to Canada along the spine of the Rocky Mountains. It's one of the most challenging long-distance trails in the world due to its varied terrain, extreme weather conditions, and the long distances between resupply points.

This is the Mount Everest of trails! Very few people have hiked this entire trail, but a kid can dream. There are countless *day hikes* and short backpacking trips you can do on the CDT, and if you're lucky, you might get to meet a thru-hiker!

Hikers that have hiked the Pacific Crest Trail, Appalachian Trail, and Continental Divide Trail are considered Tripple Crowners. A handful of hikers have even done this in one calendar year. *Wow.*

Alright, Little Explorers!

You made it to the end of this hike. Limitless possibilities lie in front of you now!

Before we part ways, I want to share some words from my heart.

In my deepest wishes and prayers, I long for a world where *clean water* and *pure air* are abundant, and where our precious ecosystems remain vibrant and unharmed.

From the enchanting hummingbirds to majestic eagles, the vital role of bees, the towering presence of ancient trees, and the meandering trails that seem to stretch into eternity, all embody the very essence of *nature's heartbeat* in our world.

It is our shared responsibility to cherish these sacred spaces and *preserve* them for generations yet to come. Let us stand together, united in our love for nature, and work hand-in-hand to relish these natural wonders and safeguard them for the future.

Iron

Further Reading

Online resources

My Website
irontazz.com

The Hiking Life
thehikinglife.com

Backpacking Light
backpackinglight.com

Leave No Trace
lnt.org

Books

I've included some adult titles here if you want to take your knowledge to the next level

NOLS Wilderness Medicine
Todd Schimelpfenig, 2021

Trail Life
Ray Jardine, 2009

Ultimate Hikers Gear Guide
Andrew Skurka, 2017

Wilderness Navigation
Bob Burns and Mike Burns, 2015

Apps

Gaia GPS
I've been using this solely for GPS for over five years now

Kindle
Great way to bring books on your trips

Sky Guide
Learn about the stars you're looking at in real time

Tides
Beyond valuable if you're hiking on the coast

This book is lovingly dedicated to Lyra, Bodhi,
and the future generations of outdoor explorers –I.T.

To my loving Jess, for taking care of me and being my
compass along the trail of making this book –M.S.

MAGIC CAT PUBLISHING

The illustrations were created digitally
Set in Noto Sans and Noyh
Library of Congress Control Number is in progress
ISBN 978-1-9155-6985-1

Text © 2024 Iron Tazz
Illustrations © 2024 Martin Stanev
Book design by Nicola Price
Edited by Jenny Broom

First published in North America in 2024 by Magic Cat Publishing, an imprint of Lucky Cat Publishing Ltd,
Unit 2, Empress Works, 24 Grove Passage, London E2 9FQ, UK

Printed and bound in Guangdong, China
10 9 8 7 6 5 4 3 2 1

Distributed by ABRAMS
195 Broadway, New York, NY 10007, USA

MIX
Paper | Supporting
responsible forestry
FSC® C104723